Starfish, Octopus, and Betta Fish

Sacha Chai

www.sachachai.com

After Naomi finished her contestant registration at the Young Ninjas Championship event, she went to see her father, Daddy Joe, before the competition started.

Naomi's face was full of worry.

"What happened, Naomi? I thought you were excited about this tournament," Daddy Joe asked.

Naomi sighed. "Yes, I did, Dad. But now that I have seen so many great ninjas here, I am not sure that I am good enough. Look over there. The boy who's doing backflips is Benjiro. He was last year's winner. He's extremely talented."

"So are you, Pumpkin!" Daddy Joe said.

"Not at his level, though," Naomi argued.

"Aww, you're anxious, Naomi. Don't worry, sweetie. Ninjas are masters of challenging tasks. We always find a way to calm down." Daddy Joe was sure proud of his ninja's traditions.

"I can't calm down when I know that my competitors are very good, Dad!" Naomi raised her voice. "I don't think I can win."

Daddy Joe knew that he had to do something before the situation got worse. "Your emotions are controlling you right now. Take a deep breath, honey. You need to have a cool head for this championship."

"Yeah, right, Dad, like I haven't tried," Naomi said.

Daddy Joe immediately thought of an old trick his mother taught him when he was young. "Whenever you're experiencing unpleasant emotions, you can quickly calm yourself down by doing the starfish, octopus, and betta fish breathing."

But grumpy little Naomi was not having it. "Starfish? No, Dad, we don't have time to go to the ocean right now."

"No, no, no. No live animals are needed here."
Daddy Joe tried not to laugh. "Just hold one of your hands
up and spread your fingers out. This is a starfish. Then, use
the other hand to trace the outline of your starfish. When
your tracing finger goes up, you breathe in. When it goes
down, you breathe out."

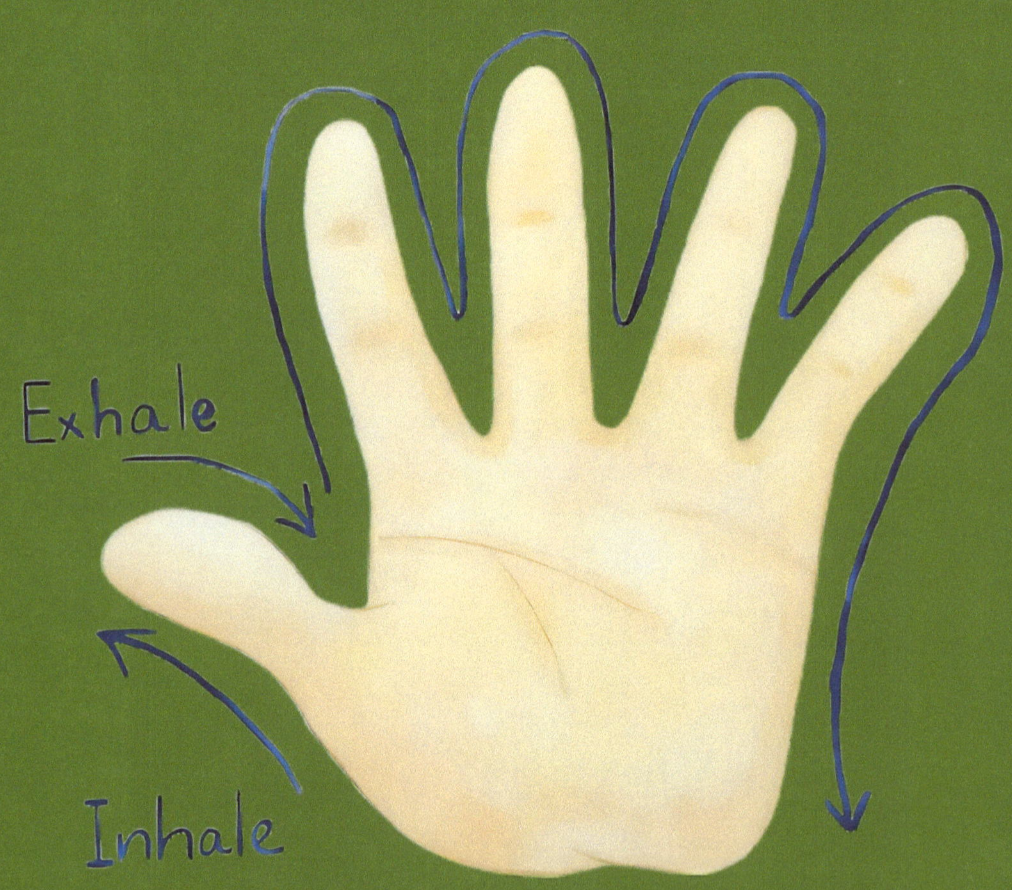

Naomi was not convinced that this silly finger-tracing thing would help, but she didn't know what else she could do. "I'll try anything at this point to bring back my sanity NOW. Alright, here we go. Up, breathe in; down, breathe out. Up, breathe in; down, breathe out. Ooh, it's kinda ticklish, Dad."

"See, you're in a better mood already. Just breathe slowly, honey." Daddy Joe demonstrated a long inhalation, followed by a much longer exhalation. "Each round gets slower and slower."

Naomi followed suit. "I am somewhat calm now, Dad. I'm calmer than I was before, that's for sure."

Daddy Joe knew what would make Naomi feel even better. "A starfish is a reminder that you're a star, baby. When you're done tracing your starfish, tell yourself, 'I was born a star. I am here to shine. And no one can dim my light.'"

Naomi repeated it after her father. Afterward, she was surprised that she felt good about herself again. Maybe this finger-tracing thing was not so silly after all, Naomi realized.

She wondered what else her father had up his sleeves.

"If you flip your hand down, you get another creature, an octopus." Daddy Joe moved his fingers back and forth to show the octopus' slimy arms.

"Oh, hello, octopus," Naomi said.

"Did you know that an octopus has nine brains?" Daddy Joe couldn't hide his excitement about this intelligent creature. "Octopuses are super smart. They are amazing problem-solvers. They can open and close jar lids, untie knots, solve mazes, disguise themselves through changing colors and shapes, recognize human faces..."

"Can octopuses help me with my math homework?"
Naomi interrupted.

35 + 81 = ?
17 - 9 = ?
8 + 12 = ?
63 - 25 = ?

"Ha, ha, ha, you wish!" Daddy Joe shook his head.
"Just flip your hand downward and trace your fingers the
same way. But for an octopus, you start tracing by
breathing out first."

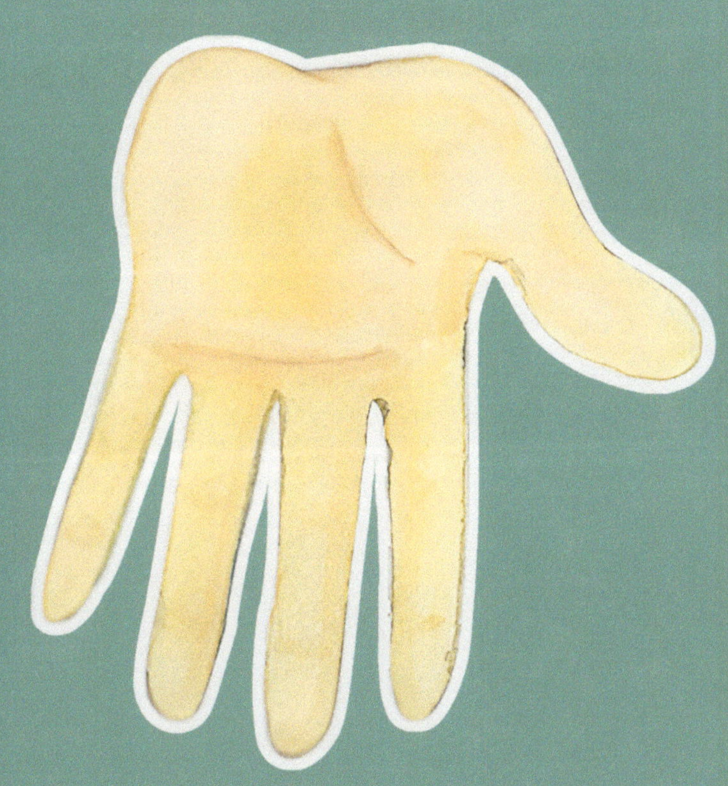

"Alright, Mr. Octopus, here I come," Naomi responded.

After Naomi had traced her octopus a few times, Daddy Joe explained further, "For octopus, you can say, 'I am smart. I can always figure things out. I can solve problems quickly.'"

Naomi repeated what her father had told her and asked, "What was the last animal you mentioned? Some kind of fish?"

Daddy Joe pulled one of his hands out of his pocket. "If you make a handshake gesture but spread your fingers out, you'll get a betta fish, which is also known as fighting fish. They are as small as the size of my thumb, but their fighting spirit is as big as the lion's. They are fearless little creatures."

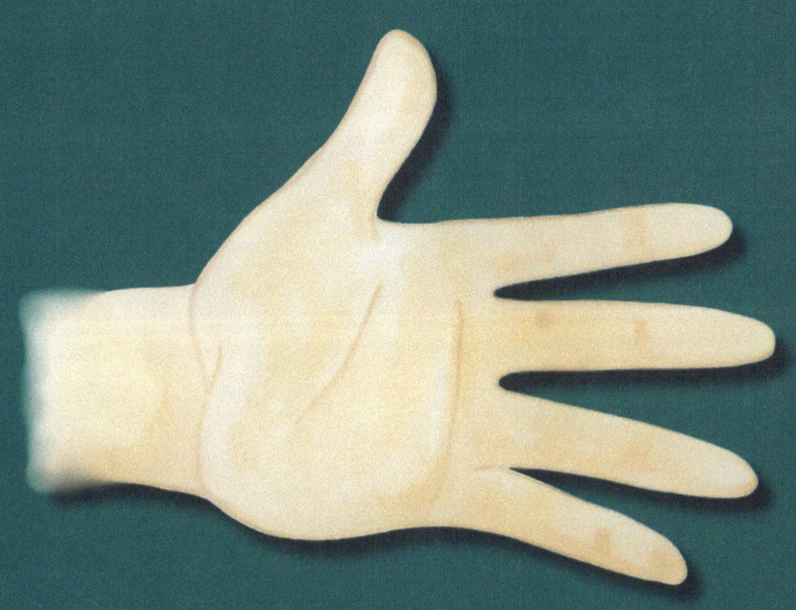

"Cool. Betta fish is my favorite animal now." Naomi adjusted the angle of her hand. "Hello there, fighting fish. You're small but mighty, just like me!"

After tracing her fingers for a few rounds, Naomi asked her father, "What do I say now? Let's have it."

"'I am a fighter. I fight for my dreams. I will not give up,'" Daddy Joe answered.

Naomi repeated after her father loudly and added, "And I am here to win!"

Daddy Joe grinned. He was glad that Naomi was already in a good mood and ready to compete. Then he tried to wrap up the conversation before she had to go. "When you experience unpleasant emotions like anger, anxiety, or worry, you can easily calm yourself down by doing the starfish, octopus, and betta fish breathing. You can do it quietly. No one needs to know. A lot of times, I keep my hands behind my back."

Suddenly, Naomi's eyes were wide open. "That's what you do when Mommy yells at you! You always put your hands behind your back! Right?"

Daddy Joe did not confirm or deny it. He just chuckled. *Smarty pants*, he thought.

After the event organizer made an announcement asking all contestants to come to the main stage, Daddy Joe gave Naomi a big hug and expressed his full confidence in her.

The challenging tasks that contestants had to compete against each other included rope climbing, star throwing, wall scaling, interpreting ninja hand signs, and underwater breathing with bamboo tubes.

However difficult those tasks might be, Naomi made it to the final round. It was not an easy feat for her.

The last task was the most difficult. It was balancing through obstacles, which included balance beams, angled steps, floating tiles, balance bridges, and spinning logs. The rules were simple: whoever could get the red flag at the finish line first would be crowned the winner, and whoever fell into the water would automatically lose. Only a few young ninjas had ever made it to the other end.

Naomi and Benjiro were the only two finalists left in the competition.

In Naomi's eyes, Benjiro seemed to be astoundingly confident. But Naomi wasn't sure if she could make it to the finish line without falling into the water, let alone beat Benjiro.

Once the final round of competition started, Naomi tried really hard to stay focused. But for a split second, she took her eyes off the obstacles to glance at Benjiro.

Plop! Naomi found both of her feet landed in the water.

So did her heart. She looked for Daddy Joe right away, trying to tell him how sorry she was.

But Daddy Joe smiled at her, raised one of his hands, and tilted it sideways.

A BETTA FISH!

Naomi immediately looked up and realized that one of her hands was still hanging onto the edge of a platform. She was still in the race!

Naomi quickly used both hands to pull herself up. Once she was back on the platform, she stared at the red flag and thrust herself toward it like her life depended on it.

Naomi focused on the flag and sped up, up, and up.
Her feet felt lighter and lighter every time she jumped.

She fogot about Benjiro.

The next thing Naomi knew, the red flag was in her
hand. She just couldn't believe her eyes!

Naomi's hand flew over her mouth. Tears started
rolling down her cheeks. She was lost for words.

Victory tasted oh so sweet, indeed.

Could you please help?

Benjiro was upset that he just lost his championship title. Could you show Benjiro how to do the starfish, octopus, and betta fish breathing to help him calm down?

Starfish, Octopus, Betta Fish
พิมพ์ครั้งแรก พฤศจิกายน พุทธศักราช 2567 จำนวน 3,000 เล่ม
National Library of Thailand Cataloging in Publication Data

Sacha Chai.
    Starfish, Octopus, and Betta Fish.-- Chiang Mai : [s.n.], 2024.
    40 p.

    1.Children's literature. I.Title.

808.068
ISBN 978-616-619-076-2

จัดพิมพ์โดย   นางสาวศศิชา วงศ์ไชย
พิมพ์ที่   อะเมซอน คินเดิล ไดเร็ค พับลิชชิ่ง
    4900 ถ.ลาครอส
    นอร์ทชาร์ลสตัน
    เซาท์แคโรไลนา
    สหรัฐอเมริกา 23406   โทร. 1-877-452-4215